P9-CRI-845

For:

From:

*This is how God showed his love among us:
He sent his one and only Son into the world
that we might live through him.*

1 JOHN 4:9

Creating *Christmas Memories*

Zondervan *Gifts*

We have a gift for inspiration™

Creating Christmas Memories:
TRADITIONS TO CELEBRATE WITH FAMILY

Copyright 1999 by ZondervanPublishingHouse
ISBN 0-310-97570-0

All Scripture quotations, unless otherwise noted, are taken from the Holy Bible: New International Version (North American Edition). Copyright 1973, 1978, 1984, by International Bible Society. Used by permission of Zondervan PublishingHouse. All rights reserved.

The NIV and New International Version trademarks are registered in the United States Patent and Trademark Office by International Bible Society.

All rights reserved. No part of this publication may be reproduced, stored in a retrieval system, or transmitted in any form or by any means-electronic, mechanical, photocopy, recording, or any other-except for brief quotations in printed reviews, without the prior permission of the publisher.

Requests for information should be addressed to:

 ZondervanPublishingHouse
Mail Drop B20
Grand Rapids, Michigan 49530
http://www.zondervan.com

Senior Editor: Gwen Ellis
Project Editor: Pat Matuszak
Designer: Garborg Design Works, Minneapolis, MN

Printed in Hong Kong

99 00 01 02 /HK/ 5 4 3 2 1

CONTENTS

CHAPTER 1

Come to the Manger

The idea of the crèche, or nativity scene, began as a way to tell the story of Jesus' birth to those who could neither read it for themselves in the Latin Bible nor understand the language of the Latin masses. The first written record of this tradition tells us that Saint Francis of Assisi organized a living manger scene for his parish in 1223. Then churches everywhere began to encourage the scenes that made the story come alive. Townspeople and parishioners gathered at the manger to sing lovely Christmas hymns. God's love could be better understood through the dramas about the birth of Christ. Nativity displays, whether of large statues or of tiny, carved figurines, made sure everyone could understand and celebrate this chronicle of God's love.

Today the tradition has become a well-loved part of the holiday season throughout the world. In France and Italy it is popular for churches to assemble miniature displays that include far more characters than the original Bible accounts name. These scenes might include peasants, villagers, artisans, children, and animals of every kind. These are scattered across an elaborate miniature countryside complete with intricate houses, farms, and roads all leading toward the stable in Bethlehem. French children also look for small ceramic nativity figures, called *santons,* that are hidden in a Christmas cake. The child who finds the *santon* is crowned with a paper crown and then gets to add the little figure to his or her personal collection or to a family display.

The Nativity Scene:
A FOCUS FOR FAMILY MEMORIES

A nativity scene is a beautiful way to celebrate the Christmas story so that young and old can delight together in the wonder of Jesus' birth!

Whether you attend a traditional holiday drama acted out under the night sky or display a set of papier-mâché nativity figurines small enough to fit on a coffee table, the nativity scene illustrates the Christmas story in a simple way that even young children can understand.

Families turn to this traditional celebration to help keep the Christ in Christmas and to help put aside all the commercial clatter that distracts from the holiday's true meaning. A nativity scene can become a focal point for family Bible reading and carol singing throughout the holiday season.

Children remember what they see, smell, and taste. A nativity scene or crèche can be their first vision of the wonder of the story of God's beautiful love for all people. A nativity set that is sturdy enough to allow children to hold the pieces and re-enact the story of the Savior's birth is an excellent way to involve their sense of touch in the learning process.

Joseph also went up from the town of Nazareth in Galilee to Judea, to Bethlehem the town of David, because he belonged to the house and line of David. He went there to register with Mary, who was pledged to be married to him and was expecting a child. While they were there, the time came for the baby to be born, and she gave birth to her firstborn, a son. She wrapped him in cloths and placed him in a manger, because there was no room for them in the inn.

And there were shepherds living out in the fields nearby, keeping watch over their flocks at night. An angel of the Lord appeared to them, and the glory of the Lord shone around them, and they were terrified. But the angel said to them, "Do not be afraid. I bring you good news of great joy that will be for all the people. Today in the town of David a Savior has been born to you; he is Christ the Lord. This will be a sign to you: You will find a baby wrapped in cloths and lying in a manger."

LUKE 2:4–12

O little town of Bethlehem, how still we see thee lie!

Above thy deep and dreamless sleep the silent stars go by.

Yet in thy dark streets shineth the everlasting Light:

The hopes and fears of all the years

Are met in thee tonight.

How silently, how silently, the wondrous gift is given!

So God imparts to human hearts the blessing of His heaven.

No ear may hear His coming, but in this world of sin,

Where meek souls will receive Him still,

The dear Christ enters in.

PHILLIP BROOKS

Bethlehem

IDEAS FOR

Consider investing in a nativity scene when your children are young. It will be a tool for teaching them the Christmas story all through their growing-up years. The crèche doesn't have to be elaborate or expensive. In fact, it is better if you are comfortable letting your children take the figures out of the manger scene to examine and play with them.

Each year as you set up your crèche, have each person choose one or more figures. As someone reads the Christmas story from the Bible, other family members can place the figures in the nativity scene.

Who can forget being chosen to play a favorite nativity character in a Sunday school Christmas pageant? Enlisting family members to put on a living nativity scene for friends and relatives or even for the whole neighborhood can be a lot of fun and can become a yearly tradition. Be sure to get photos of the event. These will become pictures to cherish.

Make a homespun nativity scene. Use a shoe box or other appropriate box for the stable and glue on hay or straw for the roof and floor. Use a felt marker to draw "boards" or "stones" on the walls of the stable, and color with brown or

FAMILY FUN

gray crayons. Use round-topped wooden clothespins for people and bits of cloth or paper for costumes. Use fine-tipped markers to draw on faces, then glue on fabric for clothing. The "legs" of the clothespins can be glued to flat wooden or cardboard squares to help them stand up in the nativity scene.

Here's a fun way to recycle Christmas cards and help young children understand the story of Jesus' birth. Cut out figures such as Mary, baby Jesus, Joseph, and the shepherds and their lambs. Glue these figures to Popsicle sticks, leaving about half the stick uncovered to serve as a handle for your stick

puppets. A curtain installed in a doorway by using a spring rod placed at waist level can be used as a puppet show stage. The children can stand behind it to act out the Christmas story. Once children understand how the story goes, let them take turns playing the part of different characters. The edge of a table or a large box can also be used for a puppet stage.

Get outside! Make a snowman nativity scene with friends and family—or if you live in the sunny climes, build a sand sculpture. Another outdoor activity is to visit local nativity displays. Join the caroling.

CHAPTER 2

A Taste of Wonder

If you have ever eaten a candy cane, you have tasted the Christmas story. Each element in this special candy's shape, color, and taste was added to tell a different part of the Christmas story. It began in the Middle Ages when mothers who wanted to calm their fidgety babies during long church masses invented pacifiers made of plain white sugar sticks. In 1670 a choirmaster in Cologne, Germany, noticed how effective the sugar sticks were and decided to bend them into cane shapes as a symbol of the Christmas shepherds' staff. He gave them as a holiday treat to the little children who sang in his choir. He found that the canes kept the children's attention focused on him as they waited for their reward. While the shape taught the children about the very first visitors to baby Jesus' manger, it also reminded them that they were singing about the birth of the Good Shepherd. When the children grew older and began to read, they noticed that when you turn the shepherds' staff upside down, it becomes a letter J, the first letter in Jesus' name.

Over the years this candy became a holiday favorite throughout Europe and America. Candy makers later added the red stripes to symbolize that Jesus was God's gift of forgiveness and love. They also put a fresh peppermint taste into the candy to stand for our lives washed clean by God's gift of grace.

The Candy Cane:

Candy canes are one holiday treat that can do more than satisfy a sweet tooth. They can help parents and grandparents tell the Christmas story in a fun way that little ones will enjoy and remember. Children love to learn in ways that use all their senses, and studies show that they remember what they are taught longer and understand it better when all of their senses are involved in the learning.

Because children can feel the candy cane's shape, see its colors, smell its fresh scent, and taste its cool, sweet flavor while they hear the Christmas story, the story becomes alive for them in a new way. Then when they are told about Jesus' birth and life, using the candy cane's symbols, they will have a story to pass on to their friends, along with a candy cane treat.

*T*aste and see that the LORD is good.

PSALM 34:8

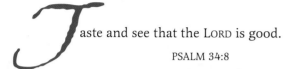

*H*ow sweet are your words to my taste,
sweeter than honey to my mouth!

PSALM 119:103

*L*ooking at his disciples, Jesus said: ...
"Blessed are you who hunger, ...
for you will be satisfied."

LUKE 6:20–21

Go tell it on the mountain,

Over the hills and everywhere.

Go tell it on the mountain

That Jesus Christ is born.

Down in a lowly manger

The humble Christ was born,

And God sent us salvation,

That blessed Christmas morn.

When I was a seeker

I sought both night and day,

I asked the Lord to help me,

And he showed me the way.

Go tell it on the mountain,

Over the hills and everywhere.

Go tell it on the mountain

That Jesus Christ is born.

SPIRITUAL

Mountain

$\mathcal{I}$DEAS FOR

What looks more at home on a Christmas tree than candy canes? And no decoration is more fun to remove! You may have trouble finding helpers to remove all the other ornaments from your tree, but candy canes seem to disappear as quickly as snowflakes in the sun. There's no cure for disappearing candy canes, so keep lots of them on hand for restocking your tree. Today, candy canes come in so many colors and sizes that you are sure to find some to match your tree's other decorations no matter what color and theme your tree has.

One of the easiest decorative shapes to cut is a candy cane. Unlike some of the more intricately shaped ornaments—snowflakes for example—you can draw the candy cane's shape onto white poster board or construction paper and cut it out. Then it is easy to glue or paint on red stripes. String a number of candy canes together with colorful yarn or ribbon to make a garland for your tree, doorway, or stair rail. Recycle last year's Christmas cards by cutting them into canes. The effect is quite colorful. Using materials other than real candy canes ensures that you will still have some candy cane ornaments when the

FAMILY FUN

real ones have all been gobbled up.

Candy cane cookies are decorations that will disappear almost as fast as the real thing, if not faster! Make your favorite sugar cookie recipe and add a few drops of peppermint flavoring and red food coloring to half of it. Children enjoy hand-rolling the dough into "snakes." Lay two snakes next to each other, one red and one without coloring. Twist the "snakes" together gently and shape them into canes. Place them on a cookie sheet and sprinkle them with sugar or crushed candy cane bits before baking. As you make the cookies, talk about the

Christian symbolism of the candy cane.

You can use a large candy cane made from felt fabric to keep track of the days until Christmas. Cut the main shape for the cane out of white felt. Make it as large as you wish. A backing of cardboard will make it stiff. Cut out a red felt stripe for each day you want to count down until Christmas. Stick the felt stripes on the cane and tack it up on a wall or refrigerator. Your candy cane hanging will look as if the stripes have been licked off as family members take turns removing one stripe each day until Christmas.

CHAPTER 3

The Christmas Tree's Tale

Long before the first written record of Christmas trees in sixteenth-century Europe, trees of all kinds were used to celebrate religious holidays. Ancient Egyptians, Romans, Chinese, Hebrews, and Celts all used trees and boughs to decorate their homes around the time of the shortest day of the year, the winter solstice. Trees have always been a symbol of life and joy during the drab days of winter.

Christian usage of the evergreen began as part of the passion plays of the Middle Ages. Because all Bibles and church sermons were in Latin, Catholic priests who wanted to teach their non-Latin-speaking congregations about the Bible often used plays to illustrate the most important stories. Paintings show that the evergreen was first used to represent the Tree of Life in the garden of Eden play, probably because it kept its green color year-round and never seemed to die out like other trees. The apples that had decorated it as part of the Garden of Eden story were kept as ornaments when German families brought the Tree of Life into their homes for Christmas. They added communion wafers and candles to the apple decorations.

Over the years many other kinds of fruit, as well as cookies and candies, were used to brighten up the tree. Later, as the tradition continued, more elaborate decorations were fashioned from blown glass. Their shapes were often those of the real fruits that had been used in the past. Glass was also blown into figures representing all of the characters from the biblical account of the nativity, so the tree still told the story of the nativity without words.

The Christmas Tree:
A FOCUS FOR FAMILY MEMORIES

A Christmas tree can be a center for family fun from the start of the holiday season to its finish. Our family fun starts when we go together to search for the perfect tree. Some of us go through snowy woods, some to tree lots set up in our neighborhood, and some of us just go up to the attic to haul down the box that has our "almost natural"

tree in it. Getting the tree is a family activity we all love. Whether it's a fresh-scented pine or a perfectly branched artificial tree, in the choosing and setting up we have reason to be together.

Many wonderful stories and milestone memories are unwrapped with each ornament we remove from tissue to hang on the tree. We remember the first ornament hung on our tree when we became a family. We find those that were handed down from parents and grandparents. We rediscover those we found on trips and brought home as reminders of our journey. We lovingly rehang the first work of art a child made and gave with delight. We remember the night we heard a strange jingling and realized it was not a reindeer on the roof but a kitten in the tree. We remember the tree that fell over and how we tied it up to keep it from falling again. We remember and we smile for the joys (and mishaps) that have come with our tree.

*M*ay the God of hope fill you with all joy and peace as you trust in him.

ROMANS 15:13

*W*orship the LORD with gladness; come before him with joyful songs.

PSALM 100:2

*W*e rejoice in the hope of the glory of God.

ROMANS 5:2

*Y*ou will go out in joy and be led forth in peace; the mountains and hills will burst into song before you, and all the trees of the field will clap their hands.

ISAIAH 55:12

O Christmas tree, O Christmas tree!

How are thy leaves so verdant!

Not only in the summertime,

But ev'n in winter is thy prime

O Christmas tree, O Christmas tree,

How are thy leaves so verdant!

O Christmas tree, O Christmas tree,

Much pleasure doth thou bring me!

For every year the Christmas tree,

Brings to us all both joy and glee

O Christmas tree, O Christmas tree,

Much pleasure doth thou bring me!

Tannenbaum

O Christmas tree, O Christmas tree,

Thy candles shine out brightly!

Each bough doth hold its tiny light,

That makes each toy to sparkle bright

O Christmas tree, O Christmas tree,

Thy candles shine out brightly!

IDEAS FOR

Many families make decorating the tree a special occasion. To help each person fully enjoy this holiday activity, think through the whole process and let each person decide which part he or she is most interested in. Adventurers and warm-blooded souls may find the tree hunt and set-up the most appealing part of the process. The detail-oriented person may unpack the ornaments with less breakage and loss than the less detailed-oriented person. Music lovers can choose songs and keep them playing as the project moves along. Nostalgia buffs might want to take photos and keep a scrapbook to record the history of each year's celebration. An artistic person might be most interested in coordinating the colors and placing the decorations on and around the tree.

What a wonderful time to remember to include family who

FAMILY FUN

can't be with you on this holiday! Photos, phone calls, or letters describing your family get-together to put up the tree are precious to relatives living far away.

Many communities have a tree-lighting ceremony on the square or at individual churches. One way to celebrate the joy of Christmas giving is to include a special giving tree for those in need. It may be a tree full of mittens of various sizes, warm winter hats, pet supplies for the local animal shelter, or a tree of stacked canned goods.

What do you do with all those stuffed animals that children outgrow so quickly? Save them for filling holes between the branches of your natural tree or hiding the center pole of your artificial one. Dress up the stuffed toys with ribbons, yarn, mittens, or sparkly garlands.

CHAPTER 4

The Symbols of Christmas

From earliest days, churches have used symbols to teach lessons from the Bible. A language of symbols was woven into tapestry, shaped into stained glass, and embroidered on priests' robes. The symbols were meant to be "read" by Christians who could not read or understand Latin. Symbols were everywhere in medieval churches, and they virtually turned a cathedral into a visual Bible that parishioners were taught from childhood to understand.

Candles are the symbol for Jesus, the Light of the World.

The manger represents the humility of Jesus. He became poor that all of humankind could become rich.

Angels stand for God's message to his people, and his special care.

A white dove is the symbol for the Holy Spirit. The dove sometimes carries an olive branch to symbolize peace on Earth.

Turtledoves represent the offering Mary and Joseph gave for Jesus' presentation at the temple.

The white rose and the poinsettia both symbolize the nativity.

The lamb stands for Jesus' sacrifice and for his people.
The shepherd symbolizes Jesus'

care and the leaders of the church.

The donkey represents patience.

Oxen or cattle symbolize strength, especially that Jesus is strong to bear our burdens.

The five-pointed star stands for God's revelation. He used a star to reveal to the wise men the birth of his Son. Christ himself is also called the Morning Star.

Gold stands for purity, for being refined by fire, and also for a gift of great value.

Frankincense and myrrh were expensive and were used for many religious ceremonies, so they symbolize holiness. Because they were used in funeral practices, they also signify Christ's sacrificial death for all humans.

The Christmas tree stands for eternal life and God's eternal love.

Christmas Symbols:

A FOCUS FOR FAMILY MEMORIES

The way we celebrate Christmas with its many stories and meanings can be just as difficult for little ones to understand as the Latin mass was for English peasants. Symbols can be a kind of shorthand for helping children focus on just one idea about Christmas at a time. Symbols can also help adults to simplify complex lives and meditate on a single facet of this beautiful season. Perhaps that is why it is so restful and inspiring to just sit and look at the lovely stained-glass windows in churches. We often grow used to looking at the stained glass windows of our churches and the symbols lose all meaning to us.

Perhaps your church building doesn't even have stained-glass windows and uses little symbolism. To focus your family's attention on the symbolism, you can go together to a cathedral or a church that does have a lot of stained glass. Go at a time of day where there are few other people there so that you can discuss the symbols with your children. All the bustle of the season will melt away under the glow of the pure colors streaming through the windows.

Families can choose their own symbols to celebrate the season. Give some thought to what has specific meaning to your family.

_T_here were shepherds living out in the fields nearby, keeping watch over their flocks at night. An angel of the Lord appeared to them. ...When the angels had left them and gone into heaven, the shepherds said to one another, "Let's go to Bethlehem and see this thing that has happened, which the Lord has told us about."

LUKE 2:8,9,15

_A_fter Jesus was born in Bethlehem in Judea, during the time of King Herod, Magi from the east came to Jerusalem and asked, "Where is the one who has been born king of the Jews? We saw his star in the east and have come to worship him." ...On coming to the house, they saw the child with his mother Mary, and they bowed down and worshiped him. Then they opened their treasures and presented him with gifts of gold and of incense and of myrrh.

MATTHEW 2:1-2, 11

The Shepherds had an Angel,

The Wise Men had a star,

But what have I, a little child,

To guide me home from far,

Where glad stars sing together,

And singing Angels are?

Christ watches me, His little lamb;

Cares for me day and night,

    That I may be His own in heaven:

So angels, clad in white,

    Shall sing their "Glory, glory"

For my sake in the height.

Lord, I will give my love to Thee,

    Than gold much costlier,

Sweeter to Thee than frankincense,

More prized than choicest myrrh;

    Lord, make me dearer day by day,

Day by day holier.

CHRISTINA ROSSETTI

IDEAS FOR

Make your own stained-glass windows. Trace and cut out shapes of Christmas symbols from black construction paper. Make two identical shapes for each symbol. Cut out the center of the shapes to leave just a frame. Cut out and sandwich a piece of colored tissue paper between the two frames and glue them together. Hang your symbols in the windows using fishing line or thin ribbons, or tape them to the window. To make your symbols last longer, you can cover each one on both sides with clear contact paper. You might want to use other symbols that are special to your family. Talk together about what animal, flower, or other symbol is special to your family and why. Each person may want to choose his or her own symbol as well.

Make stickers of your favorite Christmas symbols by using white self-adhesive labels or contact paper. Draw symbols with colored markers, or cut out symbols from last year's Christmas cards and glue them onto the paper.

This is the best time of year to tour beautiful church buildings that feature stained-glass windows. Many hold special music performances just for Christmas visitors. Many church workers will be happy

FAMILY FUN

to explain the history of their windows and the symbols used. Some churches have informational tours, and others publish booklets to help you understand and enjoy their artistic treasures. Church touring can be a fun outing for the whole family.

For edible stained glass, use your favorite sugar cookie recipe. Divide dough into two bowls. Color dough balls different colors. Cut out identical shapes of Christmas or family symbols from both colors. Trim one color of the cookie shapes about a half-inch smaller all the way around than the other color. Bake both sizes. After baking, cover the backs of the smaller cookies with your favorite frosting and stick them on top of the larger ones. The colorful edges of the larger cookies will look like the frame around a stained-glass window.

Customize your Christmas wrapping paper, using symbols. Cut symbols into a linoleum block or the flat side of a potato you have cut in half. Use stamp pad ink, acrylic paint, or poster paint of different colors to stamp symbols onto plain white or brown paper grocery bags to make gift bags. Stamp butcher paper, brown wrapping paper, or plain tissue paper to make personalized wrapping paper.

CHAPTER 5

Colors of Christmas

There is a charming folktale that is one example of the symbolism of color in the Christmas story. According to this legend, the robin was once just a plain brown bird without its bright red breast coloring. The story goes that after the wise men had visited the stable in Bethlehem, the angel warned Joseph to flee with his family to Egypt because of the evil King Herod's plot against baby boys. During their journey, Joseph built a small campfire to keep his wife and baby Jesus warm. The three went to sleep after the excitement of a long day of travel. As they slept, the fire burned low and a little, brown robin became concerned that the fire would go out. Afraid that the precious baby would become cold, the little bird came close to the fire and fanned its dying embers with its wings. As the bird stayed and kept the fire burning brightly, the feathers on his breast began to glow red in the fire's warmth, or maybe it was the warmth of his love for Jesus that made the feathers over his faithful heart glow red. The legend says that robins have proudly worn their red color ever since as a reward for this good deed.

The story is only a legend, but it gives us some idea about the symbolism of the colors we use at Christmas time. Here are some others:

Red stands for sacrifice. We remember the blood Jesus shed to save the world.

Green represents God's gift of everlasting life and hope and all the green wonders of nature he has created.

White is the symbol for God as Creator and also for light, joy, purity, and perfection.

Purple symbolizes royalty. Jesus was from the royal house of King David. Jesus was and is the King of kings.

Gold stands for glory, great worth, and virtue refined by fire.

Silver reminds us of the silver star that led the way to Bethlehem.

Christmas Colors:

A FOCUS FOR FAMILY MEMORIES

What would winter be like for us in the Northern Hemisphere without Christmas color? Imagine what we would miss if that long, dark season were never broken up by Christmas joy. The vibrant colors of Christmas make us come alive. They are a wake-up call to our sleepy senses. All those muted, autumn earth-tones fall off just like the leaves when, during Advent, Christmas colors burst forth like jewels in the snow. We can hardly wait to wrap up both our gifts and ourselves for a shining celebration.

The Christmas story is alive with colors to appreciate. The angels shine brilliant white against a black night sky. The wise men glow in their rich gold and jeweled robes. Mary, attired in her traditional blue robe, contrasts with the warm browns of the stable.

Look carefully at, and talk with your children about, the many nativity scenes on Christmas cards. There, along with the manger scene, you will find red accents such as roses. You will often find colored birds and fruit-bearing trees. See how many colors you can find! Explain that artists often painted the nati-vity scene to reflect their culture and time. Explain that this was a good idea because Jesus came to understand each one of us where we live.

The LORD their God will save them on that day
as the flock of his people.
They will sparkle in his land like jewels in a crown.
How attractive and beautiful they will be!

ZECHARIAH 9:16–17

LORD, you have assigned me my portion and my cup;
you have made my lot secure.
The boundary lines have fallen for me in pleasant places;
surely I have a delightful inheritance....
Therefore my heart is glad and my tongue rejoices;
my body also will rest secure....
You have made known to me the path of life;
You will fill me with joy in your presence,
with eternal pleasures at your right hand.

PSALM 16:5-6, 9, 11

It came upon the midnight clear,

That glorious song of old,

From angels bending near the earth

To touch their harps of gold:

"Peace on the earth, good will to men,

From heaven's all-gracious King!"

The world in solemn stillness lay

To hear the angels sing.

Still through the cloven skies they come

with peaceful wings unfurled;

and still their heavenly music floats

O'er all the weary world;

Above its sad and lowly plains

They bend on hovering wing,

And ever o'er its Babel sounds

The blessed angels sing.

EDMUND H.
SEARS

Add sprinkles of color to your dining table's centerpiece, your manger scene, or under your tree: just use a paper punch to make confetti out of old Christmas cards and wrapping paper. Sprinkle colorful bits around anywhere you want to add an accent of sparkling color. Spray the ends of the branches on your tree with a little maximum-hold hair spray, and the paper sprinkles will stick to the tree. You can also use a little spray glue. Individual bits will also stick to wet fingernail polish if you have little girls who want to dec-orate their nails or plastic hair bands for holiday fun.

Canning jars, or any leftover jars, from peanut butter to bottled fruit juice, can serve as containers to make multicolored candles. You can add color to candle wax by adding bits of leftover crayon and old candles, even old birthday candles, to the melted wax. Put the old candles and crayons into a heavy plastic bag. Crush them by hitting the bag with a meat-tenderizing hammer or rolling pin. If your leftover candles are large, try using a vegetable peeler to shave

FAMILY FUN

off strips in a spiral pattern.

When you are ready to assemble your candle, melt candle wax by placing candles in the top of a double boiler (to prevent fire). Adults must supervise this activity. Do not leave the wax unattended. Next, warm the jar by running hot water from the tap for a few minutes. Dry the jar thoroughly inside and out. Knot a string on a pencil. Place the pencil across the mouth of the jar and hang the string down inside the jar for a wick. Weighting the string will make it hang straight in the jar. Carefully pour in candle wax. Sprinkle colored bits of the crushed candle chips into the jar after you've filled it with melted paraffin. Stir with a pencil or dowel, being careful not to tangle the string wick. After the jar and wax have cooled, cut or untie the string from the pencil. Now you are ready to decorate the outside of the jar with ribbon, lace, or stickers. These colored candles can match the colors of the room you want to decorate or the room of the person who will receive it as a gift.

CHAPTER 6

Circle of Cheer

A circle has no ending or beginning, so it has long been a symbol for the eternal. When three circles are intertwined, they stand for the everlasting Trinity of Father, Son, and Holy Spirit. Evergreens were used by many cultures throughout the ages to symbolize the renewal of life and a hope for life everlasting. While the fragile leaves of most trees fall off in autumn, the hardy evergreen shows its lively color into the winter and all year long. This gave farming cultures hope that new life would return after the hardship of winter. Christians combined these two symbols, the unending circle and the evergreen, in Christmas wreaths.

Various kinds of materials used to form wreaths have historic meanings. Laurel leaves were for the victors. Holly was a sign of protection and blessing in Roman homes. It later was adopted by Christians for Christmas wreaths. In England soft, graceful ivy vines are twined together with shiny, prickly holly branches as a symbol of the way men's and women's natures balance each other. Dried grapevines twisted into wreaths remind us of the Last Supper when Jesus explained that the Passover wine was a symbol of his blood poured out to cleanse us from sin. All of these materials have been and are now used for Christmas wreaths.

A wreath can stand for both the kingship and the sacrifice of Christ. As part of his sacrifice for us, Pilate's soldiers pressed a crown of thorny vines into the temples of our Lord when they mocked him as king of the Jews.

The Christmas Wreath:

A FOCUS FOR FAMILY MEMORIES

A Christmas wreath may be the first welcome your guests receive as they approach your front door. It can be more than an announcement of joy and goodwill. It can be a devotional symbol. Both the wreath's circular shape and its evergreen materials are symbols of eternal life. You can add apples to your wreath as a symbol of life. You can add stars to remind your visitors of the Star of Bethlehem. You can add red as a symbol of Christ's sacrifice for us. When we see a Christmas wreath, we can remember that we are part of God's eternal, forever family. Our good cheer and hospitality aren't limited to one season or even to one lifetime here on Earth.

As we open our door at Christmas to beloved friends and family, our wreath can remind them to rejoice that we are meant to be together with them always, starting at this moment.

*I*n that day the LORD Almighty
   will be a glorious crown,
   a beautiful wreath
for the remnant of his people.
He will be a spirit of justice to him who sits in judgment,
a source of strength
to those who turn back the battle at the gate.

ISAIAH 28:5-6

*W*isdom will set a garland of grace on your head
   and present you with a crown of splendor.

PROVERBS 4:9

*F*or God so loved the world
   that he gave his one and only Son,
   that whoever believes in him
shall not perish but have eternal life.

JOHN 3:16

Good Christian friends, rejoice
With heart and soul and voice;
Give ye heed to what we say:
Jesus Christ is born today
Ox and ass before him bow,
And he is in the manger now,
Christ is born today!
Christ is born today.

Good Christian friends, rejoice

With heart and soul and voice;

Now ye hear of endless bliss:

Jesus Christ was born for this

He has opened heaven's door,

And we are blest forevermore,

Christ was born for this!

Christ was born for this.

Good Christian friends, rejoice

With heart and soul and voice;

Now ye need not fear the grave:

Jesus Christ was born to save.

Calls you one and calls you all,

To gain his everlasting hall,

Christ was born to save!

Christ was born to save.

TRADITIONAL GERMAN CAROL

$\mathcal{I}$DEAS FOR

It's fun to make wreaths with family and friends. We can start with an evergreen wreath and add our own touches to personalize a time-honored tradition. Plain grapevine wreaths are inexpensive and plentiful in craft stores. Or if you live in an area where grapes grow, you can make your own wreaths in the fall when you clean up vines from garden areas. After you've twisted the vines into wreaths, hang them up to dry as you wait for the Christmas season. If you don't have grapevines, use a Styrofoam base, available at most craft stores, for your wreath.

A hot-glue gun is handy for attaching the wreath greens and ornaments that have a special meaning for your family or group of friends. If you are using Styrofoam, decorations can easily be attached to the foam ring, using pins or wire.

Miniature musical instruments are often a favorite accent on wreaths. Make small drums out of used, frozen fruit juice cans. Take off the top and bottom of a washed can. Cut two circles from a piece of heavy, watermarked typing paper. Make them about one inch larger than the can's openings. Use a rubber band around

FAMILY FUN

each end to hold the paper circles in place. These paper ends are the "drum skins." Then wrap and glue a piece of plain felt or aluminum foil to the sides of the can, covering the juice label and the parts of the paper that are being held on by the rubber bands. Use ribbon or yarn to trim the drum and make a loop for hanging it on the wreath.

Got a drawer full of leftover winter scarves from past years? Why not recycle them as a colorful soft-sculpture wreath? Braid three scarves of equal length into a chain. Then coil them into a wreath and sew the ends together (or use heavy tape or flexible wire, since neither will show when the wreath is finished). If your cloth is very soft and limp, you might want to attach your wreath to a clothes hanger that you have stretched into a circle to help it keep a nice round shape. Tie a big bow made from another scarf, ribbon, or yarn over the joined ends of the wreath. Sew on any little decorations or items that follow your Christmas decorating theme and that seem to go with the colors of the scarves.

CHAPTER 7

A Song in the Night

The first carolers did more than just stand singing harmonies outside neighbors' homes at Christmas. The word *carol* comes from an Old French word that describes a folk dance done in a circle. Sometimes these caroling parties got pretty exciting—even to the point that priests in sermons warned parishioners to keep the festivity orderly and rebuked those who became too extreme in their celebration. Historically, Saint Francis of Assisi is credited with first starting the practice of singing Christmas hymns outside church buildings when he led his followers in singing at the nativity scenes he created.

The tradition of singing carols door-to-door came from an ancient Anglo-Saxon custom known as "wassailing." The word *wassail* meant to bless with good health. Originally farm families walked with their neighbors among the orchards to bless the trees for the growing season to come. They sang as they walked and they drank an apple beverage also known as wassail. When Christians adapted the wassail custom, they fellowshipped from one home to the next singing hymns about Jesus' birth. Many of them kept the custom of serving punch or other Christmas treats to their caroling neighbors.

Today choirs and carolers are welcome entertainment at indoor malls. There, in beautifully decorated surroundings that complement the singers' voices, shoppers can't help but stop their bustle and buying to listen or join in when the groups perform a favorite holiday song. For a few blessed moments strangers of all ages and races become one choir to embrace the same hope for a future of peace and a season of love.

Christmas Carols:

A FOCUS FOR FAMILY MEMORIES

Christmas is a choir that holds no auditions. Even if there is a frog in your throat or you think your singing voice sounds good only in the shower, when family or church groups are rounding folks up to form a caroling group, there are no excuses good enough to keep you out. Friends and family just want you to join in, to make a joyful noise, no matter how humble your talents. For most caroling groups, the rule seems to be, the more voices, the better. There is nothing that joins hearts together like a song sung under the stars on a holiday stroll with family and friends. It's a wonderful way to welcome new neighbors and to get to know others you've somehow never met. When people open their doors with a delighted smile or stop in a bustling mall to join in a chorus of their favorite song, it's a testimony of the way that God's gift of his Son opens the doors of our hearts during this special season. So make a loud noise and rejoice in praises to God!

My servants will sing
out of the joy of their hearts.

Isaiah 65:14

Give thanks to the LORD, call on his name;
make known among the nations what he has done.
Sing to him, sing praise to him;
tell of all his wonderful acts.
Glory in his holy name;
let the hearts of those who seek the LORD rejoice.
Look to the LORD and his strength;
seek his face always.
Remember the wonders he has done.

1 Chronicles 16:8–12

Joy to the world! the Lord is come:

Let Earth receive her King;

Let every heart prepare Him room,

And heaven and nature sing,

And heaven and nature sing,

And heaven, and heaven and nature sing.

Joy to the world! the Savior reigns;

Let men their songs employ;

While fields and floods, rocks, hills, and plains

Repeat the sounding joy,

Repeat the sounding joy,

Repeat, repeat the sounding joy.

He rules the world with truth and grace,

And makes the nations prove

The glories of His righteousness,

And wonders of His love,

And wonders of His love,

And wonders, and wonders of His love.

ISAAC WATTS

Many children enjoy the activity of caroling and joining in the children's choirs as they busily prepare for Christmas pageants and concerts. There always seems to be an open spot for one more willing volunteer. Encourage your children to get involved, for whether they are out in the spotlight on the stage or engaged in some supportive activity behind the scenes, they will learn and grow. These activities can stretch the imagination and even turn up undiscovered interests in music, art, or public speaking. It adds to the fun of sharing at Christmas if children have a

chance to visit other churches where school friends may be performing.

Make a tape or video recording of your family singing favorite carols, to send to relatives who live too far away to be with you during the holidays. Grandparents, aunts, and uncles who live across the country will appreciate seeing how much your children have grown and how sweetly they sing. You can include reading the Christmas story as the family camera operator scans the group, or have each person take a turn reading a portion of the story. Years later children will still ask to

FAMILY FUN

see the video of themselves or their parents.

Do the children at your house know the words to all the Christmas carols they love to sing? When we see them enthusiastically joining in, we might feel sure they do. But when we quiet everyone else down long enough to listen to what individual children are singing, the result can be both surprising and humorous. Here are some unusual versions of favorite carols from boys and girls who learned to sing them without following the hymnbook. See if your children have their own little gems that you haven't heard before.

Angel cats that purred on high...

Angel's sleeve that's furred and high...

Angels, we have served the pie...

Go spill it on the mountain...

holy night, the cars are brightly shining...

Gloria...In eggshells see day glows...

Deck the halls with Buddy Holly...

little clown of Bethlehem, how silly seaweed high...

Noel, noel, noel, noel... Barney's the king of his tale.

Round John Virgin, mother, and child...

CHAPTER 8

Christmas Bells

The first mention of bells in the Bible is found in God's direction to Moses about how to make a ceremonial robe for the priests of Israel. He told Moses to put bells on the hem of the priests' garments so they would jingle when the priests ministered behind the thick curtain where the presence of God stayed. The people in the congregation could hear the priest moving around and knew that he was offering a sacrifice in the Holy Place.

Just as bells in the temple signaled the forgiveness of sins for the Israelites, bells have been used over the centuries to let communities know that something important was happening. When leaders wanted to gather their people together in one place, whether for the joy of announcing an important treaty or an upcoming wedding or to prepare for an attack by an enemy or to fight a fire, they rang big bells so everyone could be called at once.

One legend tells of a blind beggar boy in Bethlehem who heard that shepherds had told everyone about a choir of angels who came to announce that the King of Israel was born and that they would find him sleeping in a manger in one of the town's stables. The boy pleaded with passersby to take him to the baby, but everyone ignored his requests and rushed on their way. As the night grew dark and silent, the little boy could faintly hear the sound of a cow's bell somewhere nearby. He wondered who was keeping a cow awake so late at night. Then he realized that the reason the cow was stirring might be a baby and its family staying in the stable. Maybe the cow had to stretch its neck way out to eat hay because the family was using the manger as a bed for their new baby! Maybe *that's* why the bell was tinkling! He carefully made his way through the streets, following the sound of the bell, until it led him to a stable where he heard a mother singing a lullaby. He knew then that he had found the newborn King, thanks to a special Christmas bell.

The Bells of Christmas:

A FOCUS FOR FAMILY MEMORIES

The sound of bells is the sound of Christmas. The jingle of bells tells us that the horse and carriage, all decorated for the season, is coming around the corner or a shop door is being opened or a sidewalk kettle is receiving a holiday donation. The clear tone of church bells calls us to celebrate together or announces the glad tidings of Noel without a word being spoken.

Our lives can ring out a clear message to all we meet throughout the year when we show others God's love and joy. We don't need a lot of time to show people that God loves them. We don't need to preach to tell others that our lives are changed because of his Gift. Just as people look in curiosity to see why a bell is ringing, they will be curious about why our lives ring with God's true Spirit. We are like the Christmas bells that call others to come and see what God has done.

henever Aaron enters the Holy Place, he will bear the names of the sons of Israel over his heart. Make the robe of the ephod entirely of blue cloth. Make pomegranates of blue, purple and scarlet yarn around the hem of the robe, with gold bells between them. The gold bells and the pomegranates are to alternate around the hem of the robe. Aaron must wear it when he ministers. The sound of the bells will be heard when he enters the Holy Place before the LORD and when he comes out.

EXODUS 28:29,31,33,33-35

On that day HOLY TO THE LORD will be inscribed on the bells of the horses.

ZECHARIAH 14:20

I heard the bells on Christmas day

Their old familiar carols play

And mild and sweet the words repeat,

Of peace on earth, good will to men.

I thought how as the day had come,

The belfries of all Christendom

Had roll'd along the unbroken song

Of peace on earth, good will to men.

And in despair I bow'd my head:

"There is no peace on earth," I said,

"For hate is strong, and mocks the song

Of peace on earth, good will to men."

Then pealed the bells more loud and deep:

"God is not dead, nor doth He sleep;

The wrong shall fail, the right prevail,

With peace on earth, good will to men."

'Til ringing, singing on its way,

The world revolved from night to day,

A voice, a chime, a chant sublime,

Of peace on earth, good will to men!

HENRY WADSWORTH LONGFELLOW

IDEAS FOR

Everyone enjoys the sound of jingling bells at Christmas. Hang them on an outside door, attached to a leather or felt strap or around the doorknob with a circle of twine or ribbon. You can even put a lot of them together as a wreath or add a few of them to an existing wreath. The jingle announces that guests have arrived and lets them feel specially welcomed. Children like to ring a silvery bell to gather the family for dinner or dessert. One mom confessed that she hung jingle bells on her children's bedroom doors so she would hear them if they came sneaking down to catch her putting presents under the tree on Christmas Eve! Another sewed bells on her new kitten's collar, to serve as a warning when kitty was getting curious about the Christmas tree or the electrical cords running to it.

A fun stocking stuffer is a pair of jingle bell gloves. Sew small round bells, available at craft stores, to mittens or the finger ends of gloves. Children and adults will have fun waving and jingling a Christmas hello at the same time.

FAMILY FUN

Many churches have special performances by bell choirs at Christmas. They may give educational talks about how various bells provide the beautiful music together and how bell ringers change the sound for different songs. Videotapes of Christmas music often feature bell choirs. Others might feature the grand steeple bells of cathedrals so you can enjoy their clear notes right in your own home.

Every year, bell ringers for local charities collect cash donations for the needy. Here is an opportunity to let your children know that giving is the heart of Christmas. It doesn't have to be a large amount, but put something into the collection pot every time you go to the store, and let your children put in a contribution as well. Some families even take time to help by volunteering to ring the bell. Whole families pass the bell from one member to the next to inspire their neighbors to give to a charity they feel is important.

CHAPTER 9

Angels We Have Heard

In the Christmas story angels were actively involved in the events. They made absolutely earth-shaking announcements, then calmed the people who heard and directed them to take action.

First there was Gabriel's announcement to Mary. He let her know that God loved her, then told her God's astonishing plan for her life. He calmed her fears, and his words inspired her to trust God to make the plan come about.

Then an angel spoke to Joseph in a dream and took away all his fears as well. And later on another angel warned Joseph to take the baby Jesus and his mother Mary to Egypt where they would be safe from harm.

But it was to the shepherds that the largest group of angels appeared over their sleepy pastures. They were very frightened. These shepherds, the first who heard about the birth of God's Son, may have been just children themselves, as the job of shepherding often falls to the youngest in Israeli families. The angels gently calmed their fears. The shepherds were inspired and directed by the angels' message and went right to Bethlehem to find the baby they had heard about.

We get the feeling that angels were just a breath away from appearing to anyone in the nativity story. Their loving warmth seems to embrace the manger and its little group of family and friends like protective arms. When evil threatened to break in upon the happy scene, an angel came to Joseph again in a dream to warn him about the jealous plans of King Herod. The angel's comforting words let Joseph know that if he obeyed the directions they brought him from God, his family would escape harm.

Angels:

A FOCUS FOR FAMILY MEMORIES

Angels do many important jobs in God's kingdom. In the Bible we see angels bringing special messages, helping God's people when they are in trouble, and inspiring them to do God's will. And we may know only a small part of all the work angels do.

Some people in our lives are a lot like angels. They help us understand God's will, work behind the scenes to help us, and are examples that give us the strength to do what is right. Sometimes these people sit right at our dinner table! Look around. Has someone sitting next to you been an encouragement to you? Do you wish you could give that person an angel wings award for all the help he or she has given you? Could you be an "angel" to someone else? Is there someone who could use some special help that you could give?

od sent the angel Gabriel to Nazareth, a town in Galilee, to a virgin pledged to be married to a man named Joseph,... The angel went to her and said, "... Do not be afraid, Mary, you have found favor with God. You will be with child and give birth to a son, and you are to give him the name Jesus."

LUKE 1:26–28, 30–31

ary was pledged to be married to Joseph, but before they came together, she was found to be with child through the Holy Spirit. Because Joseph her husband was a righteous man and did not want to expose her to public disgrace, he had in mind to divorce her quietly. But after he had considered this, an angel of the Lord appeared to him in a dream and said, "Joseph son of David, do not be afraid to take Mary home as your wife, because what is conceived in her is from the Holy Spirit. She will give birth to a son, and you are to give him the name Jesus, because he will save his people from their sins."

MATTHEW 1:18--21

hen the wise men had gone, an angel of the Lord appeared to Joseph in a dream. "Get up," he said, "take the child and his mother and escape to Egypt. Stay there until I tell you, for Herod is going to search for the child to kill him." So he got up, took the child and his mother during the night and left for Egypt, where he stayed until the death of Herod.

MATTHEW 2:13–15

Angels we have heard on high,

Sweetly singing o'er the plains,

And the mountains in reply

Echoing their joyous strains.

Gloria, in excelsius Deo.

Shepherd why this jubilee?

Why your joyous strains prolong?

What the gladsome tidings be,

Which inspire your heavenly song?

Gloria, in excelsius Deo.

Come to Bethlehem and see

Him whose birth the angels sing;

Come adore, on bended knee,

Christ, the Lord, the newborn King.

Gloria, in excelsius Deo.

TRADITIONAL FRENCH CAROL

Christmas is a wonderful time for looking for the best in others. If someone in your life has been a blessing to you, why not tell that person, "I see an angel in you and your good work"? A warm thank-you or card of appreciation can light someone else's day. Don't forget to thank children for the little things they do. They will remember and learn by your example to show appreciation.

In the classic movie favorite, *It's a Wonderful Life*, one of the little girls in the family excitedly tells her father, "Every time a bell rings, an angel gets its wings." To make a special thank-you for angels who've blessed your life, cut out a small pair of wings from lace, felt, leftover Christmas cards, or construction paper. Glue a small jingle bell onto the front and write "Thank you" on the back. You can string a piece of gold or silver trim ribbon through the top to make a hanger for it, or you can pin it to your "angel's" clothing.

Help children make an angel coupon book to give to friends and family. Write "Angel Coupon" at the top of several small sheets of colored construction paper. Underneath

FAMILY FUN

write: "Call me when you need an angel to help you by_____." Leave a blank after the last words in the sentence. Discuss ways children can be helpers throughout the year. Discuss to whom they would like to give the coupons. Help them fill in the blank.

Angels in the Bible were often so majestic and beautiful in appearance that people who saw them were astonished, but these amazing beings always gave the glory to God, even when they had done something spectacular in the sight of others. Think of reasons to be thankful for the gifts God has given you that have enabled you to be a blessing to others.

Angelic appearances were often secret and surrounded by mystery in the Bible. Want to add some mystery to your Christmas season? Be a "secret angel" to someone who needs encouragement or delight. Do a good deed or leave an encouraging note or Bible verse where he or she will find it, then write, "From your secret angel" as your signature.

CHAPTER 10

Shepherds Came to See

One of Jesus' best-loved parables is about the good shepherd. Jesus tells his disciples that those who love God will be just as drawn to his voice as the little lambs are drawn to the call of the shepherd who feeds them. It's a love relationship in which the patient shepherd takes care of his flock day after day and they become loyal to follow his voice, and his voice only. When one of those sheep gets lost, he will faithfully search to find it, even though he has many more sheep.

One of the most repeated symbols in the Bible is the shepherd. To help people in Israel understand what God is like, Jesus compared himself to a shepherd, someone who had one of the most common jobs in the community. Shepherds could be seen most anywhere. The whole community depended upon the shepherd to faithfully care for the sheep. But even though the people needed the shepherds, shepherds weren't highly esteemed. The people needed their labors but didn't give them honor or riches for doing their job. Shepherds were often young children, as David was when he shepherded his father's flock.

But in spite of the beautiful, pastoral settings in which shepherds are often painted, their job often required great courage. When God sent David to fight Goliath, David already had some practical combat training in battles against a lion and a bear. David knew God had given him the strength to kill both predators even though he was only a boy. So when David faced the giant he felt confident that he could once again conquer through God's strength. The good shepherd is a portrait of both the power and gentleness of God's love.

Shepherds:
A FOCUS FOR FAMILY MEMORIES

Just as we may entertain angels unaware at our dinner table, we may not notice the shepherds who live right in our own homes. The shepherds among us are those who take care of the practical details of life from day to day. They are the ones who make sure our families are cared for. They watch out for danger and plan for the future. They are patiently thankful for the ordinary provisions of sunshine and silent streams in peaceful valleys.

Shepherds may be astonished at the unexpected miracles of God, but they know what to do next when they see a miracle: go tell everyone! And people listen when a quiet shepherd has something to say. The people in Bethlehem believed the shepherds' story about seeing a heavenly host of angels, because they knew those steady, caring shepherds could be trusted not to overreact. If the shepherds were excited, everyone else should get excited, too!

*W*hen the angels had left them and gone into heaven, the shepherds said to one another, "Let's go to Bethlehem and see this thing that has happened, which the Lord has told us about." So they hurried off and found Mary and Joseph, and the baby, who was lying in the manger. When they had seen him, they spread the word concerning what had been told them about this child, and all who heard it were amazed at what the shepherds said to them.

LUKE 2:15–18

*H*e will stand and shepherd his flock in the strength of the LORD, in the majesty of the name of the LORD his God. And they will live securely, for then his greatness will reach to the ends of the earth. And he will be their peace.

MICAH 5:4–5

O come, all ye faithful,

Joyful and triumphant,

O come ye, O come ye to Bethlehem;

Come and behold Him,

Born the King of angels;

O come, let us adore Him,

O come, let us adore Him,

O come, let us adore Him,

Christ the Lord.

Sing, choirs of angels,

Sing in exultation,

O Sing, all ye citizens of heaven above;

Glory to God,

All glory in the highest:

O come, let us adore Him,

O come, let us adore Him,

O come, let us adore Him,

Christ the Lord.

Yea, Lord, we greet Thee,

Born this happy morning;

O Jesus, to Thee be all glory given;

Word of the Father,

Now in flesh appearing:

O come, let us adore Him,

O come, let us adore Him,

O come, let us adore Him,

Christ the Lord.

TRADITIONAL HYMN, TRANSLATED FROM LATIN BY F. OAKLEY, 1841

Shepherds know their sheep well. They keep track of each sheep's progress, just as we keep track of each family member's growth. Christmas is a time to remember the days when our grown-up sheep were only little lambs. When your family gathers, bring out both the photo albums and the stories that go with each cherished picture. Take some time to remember the small things that have made your life together special. The best stories are the real ones.

Make sure your little lambs don't get lost in the bustle of Christmas. Each child has a special gift to contribute to your celebration. One will have a reading, another a song, and a third a picture he or she has made. You won't find better entertainment or decorations at the Ritz!

Shepherds not only look back and remember their flock's growth; they look to the future to decide where their sheep are headed. A great tool not only for looking back

FAMILY FUN

but also for looking forward is a Christmas memory book. It can include plans for the future, dreams to hang our hopes on, and prayer requests for the coming year. Individual family members can volunteer to be each other's prayer partners about specific matters, or each person can write a prayer request on a piece of paper, put it in a box, and then draw out another's request. Promise to pray about the request regularly and to send the person who made the request encouraging Scripture and thoughts throughout the year.

Sheep get very hungry and shepherds are the ones who have to provide the eats! Exchange recipes with other family members at Christmas and pass on those favorite cooking tips to the next generation. Don't let teenagers beg off when it's time to prepare food. They can learn a lot by assisting in the cooking.

CHAPTER 11

A Star to Light the Way

The clear light and predictable patterns of stars have led seafaring cultures for hundreds of years, but at the birth of Jesus, a new star appeared that was very different from all the other planets, comets, and heavenly lights. It is rather surprising that only a small band of wise men noticed and followed it. Perhaps they were the only ones who took time to look up at the right moment.

In his book *The Miracle of Christmas: God with Us,* John MacArthur openly wonders about the Christmas star:

"Every Christmas the planetariums and astronomers offer explanation of the Christmas star. Some say it must have been Jupiter, or a comet, or the conjunction of two planets, or some other natural phenomenon. None of those explanations is plausible, because the star led them right to the house where Jesus was. No known natural occurrence could have done that.

What was the star? No one knows, and Scripture doesn't say, but the biblical phenomenon that most closely resembles it is the Shekinah glory, the visual expression of God's glory, which in the time of Moses led Israel to the Promised Land, appearing as a pillar of cloud by day and a pillar of fire by night (Exodus 13:21). It was the same glory that shone on the shepherds when they learned of Christ's birth (Luke 2:9). Perhaps what the Magi saw was a similar manifestation of God's glory, which appeared to them like a star."

Star of Wonder:
A FOCUS FOR FAMILY MEMORIES

Stars are an important part of Christmas. A special star led the wise men to Bethlehem. Jesus is called the Morning Star that rises to give light in our hearts when we believe. We need to remember that Christmas joy doesn't necessarily flow from our homes because we are especially nice people. It is a result of making Jesus Christ the light we choose to follow above all others. It's easy for outsiders to think that we Christians just don't have any serious problems or that we are just "good" people. If we catch others making this assumption about our "nice" homes, we need to point them to the Light whose strength keeps our homes together. Those who follow his star also lead others.

rise, shine, for your light has come,
and the glory of the LORD rises upon you.
See, darkness covers the earth
and thick darkness is over the peoples,
but the LORD rises upon you
and his glory appears over you.
Nations will come to your light,
and kings to the brightness of your dawn.

ISAIAH 60:1-3

"Surely you will summon nations you know not,
and nations that do not know you will hasten to you,
because of the LORD your God,
the Holy One of Israel, for he has endowed
you with splendor," says the Lord.
Seek the LORD while he may be found;
call on him while he is near.

ISAIAH 55:5-6

"I will lead the blind by ways they have not known,
along unfamiliar paths I will guide them;
I will turn the darkness into light before them
and make the rough places smooth.
These are the things I will do;
I will not forsake them," says the LORD.

ISAIAH 42:16

star will come out of Jacob;
a scepter will rise out of Israel.

NUMBERS 24:17

The first Noel the angel did say

Was to certain poor shepherds in fields as they lay:

In fields where they lay a-keeping their sheep

On a cold winter's night that was so deep.

They looked up and saw a star,

Shining in the east, beyond them far:

And to the earth it gave great light,

And so it continued both day and night.

And by the light of that same star

Three wise men came from the country far;

To seek for a King was their intent,

And to follow the star wherever it went.

The First Noel

This star drew nigh to the northwest;

O'er Bethlehem it took its rest,

And there it did both stop and stay,

Right over the place where Jesus lay.

Then let us all with one accord

Sing praises to our heavenly Lord,

That hath made heaven and earth of naught,

And with his blood mankind has bought.

Noel, Noel, Noel, Noel

Born is the King of Israel.

OLD ENGLISH CAROL

Take time to look at the winter stars together. A neighborhood walk or time together on a porch or even peeking through a window from the warmth of a darkened house can open up a quiet time for heartfelt fellowship. There is something about looking up at the stars that opens us to the vastness of God's creation. When God wanted Abraham to understand his promises, he pointed out to his faithful friend the number of stars in the sky. And remember as you walk that a special star announced Christ's birth.

Planetariums often set up special Christmas presentations. These can be educational and interesting events and may give us an opportunity to meet others who are looking up to the heavens to learn of a God who cares for them.

Search the Internet for Web

FAMILY FUN

sites with information about stars and planets. These pages contain a lot of photos, so have patience to allow your computer to load them before you move the mouse around.

We put lights on our Christmas trees and outside on our houses to remind us of stars. From a simple string of lights to an intricate lighted topiary, lights say we are all seekers of wonder at Christmas.

Put a star on the top of your tree to remind your family that Christ the Lord was announced by a star. You may even want to make a star for the top of your tree. Let your children help.

CHAPTER 12

Wise Men Still Seek

Bethlehem was dwarfed by the huge fortress King Herod had built on its horizon. His grand palace cast a shadow over this tiny town of about 250 people.

The bloodthirsty Herod reigned as a merciless tyrant who was troubled by the small village that prophecy had declared would be the birthplace of the true King of Israel. Therefore every baby boy born in Bethlehem was a possible threat to Herod's throne. He knew his oppressed people were watching eagerly for a merciful deliverer. Even though Herod had constructed a new temple and tried to win the priests' approval of his power, when the mysterious kings from the east appeared and wanted to know where Hebrew prophets said the Messiah would be born, Herod was afraid. The prophecy said:

"You, Bethlehem Ephrathah, though you are small among the clans of Judah, out of you will come for me one who will be ruler over Israel, whose origins are from of old, from ancient times" (Micah 5:2).

How could these foreigners know about a new king? Their appearance caught Herod off guard. He thought only the zealots of Israel were concerned with God's doings. He thought his wicked rule was a secret kept in his own lands and under his own control. How had these pagan scholars learned about the obscure legend of a coming king? Suddenly it was as though truth had escaped his power and would soon be known everywhere.

Herod wanted to send the wise men as spies into Bethlehem to bring him news of the conspirators who would take his throne away. But God warned the Magi of Herod's evil plan in a dream. They left Bethlehem without reporting back to him at all.

Wise Seekers:
A FOCUS FOR FAMILY MEMORIES

The wise men who came to the manger were known as masters of so much mystical knowledge that they were called "magi" or "magicians." The Magi had gained enough wealth and power by their wisdom to also be known as kings. They stopped at the palace of King Herod, to ask about the baby that they thought the star was foretelling. These kings were not of God's chosen people. But they sought for the King and they showed us Jesus came to draw

people of all nations to God.

Others who come to our homes may be seeking the King of kings. We need to be sensitive to point the way not only to the manger but also to the cross when our guests ask a reason for the hope that is in us: "In your hearts set apart Christ as Lord. Always be prepared to give an answer to everyone who asks you to give the reason for the hope that you have. But do this with gentleness and respect" (1 Peter 3:15).

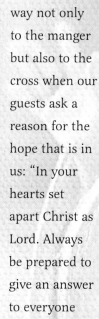

*M*agi from the east came to Jerusalem and asked, "Where is the one who has been born king of the Jews? We saw his star in the east and have come to worship him." ... and the star they had seen in the east went ahead of them until it stopped over the place where the child was. When they saw the star, they were overjoyed.... They saw the child with his mother Mary, and they bowed down and worshiped him. Then they opened their treasures and presented him with gifts of gold and of incense and of myrrh.

MATTHEW 2:1–2, 9–11

We three kings of Orient are;

Bearing gifts, we traverse afar,

Field and fountain, moor and mountain,

Following yonder star.

O star of wonder, star of night,

Star with royal beauty bright,

Westward leading, still proceeding,

Guide us to Thy perfect light.

Born a King on Bethlehem's plain,

Gold I bring to crown Him again,

King forever, ceasing never,

Over us all to reign.

O star of wonder, star of night,

Star with royal beauty bright,

Westward leading, still proceeding,

Guide us to Thy perfect light.

JOHN HENRY HOPKINS

IDEAS FOR

Christmas can be the best time to reach out to seekers in your community and show God's love to those whose hearts are as hungry for truth today as were the wise men's hearts of long ago. Here are some ideas for seeking out seekers.

Local colleges have lists of foreign students who are studying in the United States and will not be able to go home at Christmastime. These students would welcome a home-cooked meal over the holidays. Give your family an opportunity to be a host so Jesus' words, "I was a stranger and you took me in...." can come true in your home this year.

Many churches and community groups organize Christmas meals, along with carol singing and presents for the elderly in local nursing homes. Your family can work together to put on a celebration or send gifts of food, homemade

FAMILY FUN

cards, or presents to make the season cheerier for those who might otherwise spend it alone.

Community businesses, hospitals, prisons, police stations, libraries, and bookstores often appreciate homemade decorations at Christmas. Some have rules about using religious symbols, but others are open to biblical displays and embrace the spiritual message of Christmas in a way that wouldn't be allowed during other times of the year.

Reading Christmas stories aloud can be a fun way to reach seekers and is an outreach that will be welcomed with open arms. Offer to read inspirational children's books at stores, at libraries, or in the seating areas of malls. You might be the first one to tell a child about the real meaning of Christmas through your reading.

CHAPTER 13

Christmas Eve

The night before Christmas may be the world's most anticipated annual event. Long ago, Israel anticipated the arrival of Messiah. The people carefully read the Old Testament prophecies concerning where Jesus would be born and the circumstances that would lead to his coming. His star, his ancestors, his flight into Egypt to escape Herod were all mentioned in holy writings long before he came. For Israeli parents, every new baby boy born to them might be the One who would deliver Israel from her hard bondage to foreign kings. Two thousand years later we can still feel the anticipation as we light Advent candles in the weeks before Christmas. We still get excited as we count down the days with special calendars. We still have hope of his coming as we send cards, prepare special meals, and put up decorations.

In many countries Christmas Eve is the time for the big family dinner and opening gifts. In Poland the most significant rituals are celebrated on this day, called Wagilia. The Gwiadorze, or star carriers, stroll through villages. Some sing carols, others recite verses or perform puppet shows, and still others perform nativity scenes. The star carriers can also be seen in the streets of Alaska, where they are chased by participants dressed up to look like King Herod's soldiers. The soldiers try to capture the star.

In Holland farmers blow long horns at sunset to announce the coming of Christmas. In Greece small boys sing and play drums to welcome Christmas Eve, while in Switzerland and Germany the Christkind, dressed in a white robe and crown, visits homes, bearing gifts. In the south of France a large Yule log is lit in the fireplaces of grand old châteaus. Around the globe, bells ring to call faithful Christians to midnight church services. And in some places every kind of noisemakers, from fireworks to firearms, are set off to let folks know the celebration has begun.

Christmas Eve

A FOCUS FOR FAMILY MEMORIES

The night before Christmas is traditionally a night for gathering families and church members to begin the celebration of Christmas the next morning. Candlelight services or family traditions with special meanings add to the joy of this night of God's miracle. Some families have Christmas dinner and open gifts on Christmas Eve,

and others wait until Christmas Day. Airlines know there will be a rush before Christmas as everyone tries to get home on or before Christmas Eve to be with loved ones throughout the holiday season.

Christmas legends from many different countries surround the evening before the wondrous day when God's own Son became one of the sons of men. Some say that animals are given the gift of speech at midnight on Christmas Eve. Others tell of mysterious visitors who leave presents in the tradition of the Magi, and there are even stories that some trees bloom only at midnight on Christmas Eve. Stories that celebrate the mystery and anticipation of that first Noel are fun to hear when they don't crowd out the true meaning of Jesus' birth.

*C*omfort, comfort my people,
says your God.
Speak tenderly to Jerusalem,
and proclaim to her
that her hard service has been completed,
 that her sin has been paid for,
that she has received from the LORD's hand double for all her sins.
A voice of one calling:
"In the desert prepare
the way for the LORD;
make straight in the wilderness
a highway for our God.
Every valley shall be raised up,
every mountain and hill made low;
the rough ground shall become level,
the rugged places a plain.
And the glory of the LORD will be revealed,
and all mankind together will see it.
For the mouth of the LORD has spoken."

Isaiah 40:1–5

Silent Night

Silent night! holy night!

All is calm, all is bright

round yon virgin mother and child,

Holy infant so tender and mild,

sleep in heavenly peace!

Silent night! holy night!

Shepherds quake at the sight;

glories stream from heaven afar,

heavenly hosts sing Alleluia,

Christ, the Savior, is born!

Silent night! holy night!

Son of God, love's pure light

radiant beams from thy holy face,

with the dawn of redeeming grace,

Jesus, Lord at thy birth.

JOSEPH MOHR

IDEAS FOR

Since Christmas is the number one holiday for visiting family, it's also the best chance we get to make memories together. Some families go to churches that hold beautiful candlelight services, while others find it more valuable to just stay at home and be together as a family.

Whatever your family enjoys doing together will be cherished in the years to come. It doesn't have to be elaborate. Favorite board games, stories, or songs around a fireplace or Christmas tree will create warm moments to remember. Some families let each person open one gift on Christmas Eve, but others make a game of guessing what's in the packages and then waiting until Christmas Morning to find out who guessed right.

A fun activity is stringing popcorn or puffed cereal and hanging it outside for the birds. Children love to look out a window and see birds and squirrels eating treats on Christmas Morning. One way to give birds a true Christmas bonanza is to coat pinecones with peanut butter and roll them in mixed birdseed. The peanut butter has good protein, and it causes the seeds to

FAMILY FUN

stick long enough for the birds to have a feast.

Small children can have fun stringing together empty thread spools. Give them a piece of brightly colored yarn to thread through the center hole of the spools. Wrap a piece of tape at the end of the yarn, and little ones won't need to use a needle for threading. They might like to decorate the spools with stickers, crayons, or bits and pieces of lace and ribbon glued on. Let them decorate their garlands any way they choose. It will be beautiful to them. Uncooked,

wheel-shaped macaroni and buttons with large holes are also easy for little fingers to thread as a Christmas garland.

Trace the hands or feet of your youngsters onto construction paper or the back of leftover wrapping paper. String the shapes together with yarn to make a whimsical garland. If you save these tracings from year to year, you will have a growth record for each of your children. If you'd like your tracings to last, cover them with clear contact paper.

CHAPTER 14

Christmas Morning

We choose our words with wit and care.
We practice sermons to the air.
We send out writing everywhere
But God became a baby.

We try our best to be profound.
We listen, and we like the sound
Of our own voices, full and round,
but God became a baby.

The truth is simple, brave and bold.
The truth needs only to be told.
"Just as I am" ~ the story's old.
Our God became a baby.

JOY JACOBS

Jesus became the King for all time. There was no gold bright enough to honor his majesty, nor was there a scepter regal enough to confirm him as King. He did not come to sit upon a gilded throne and reign as an earthly king. Instead he took for his throne the green hillsides of Israel and for his scepter a shepherd's staff. That is why the greatest celebrations to honor his birth are not those that cost huge amounts of money, but those that recognize the eternal embrace of God's love.

Everyone is like a child at Christmas. We wonder what special secrets are wrapped in bows and sparkly paper, what gifts of sweet candy and bright toys await under a shining Christmas tree. We wait with expectancy for the wonderful surprises that will be unveiled as wrappings are torn away and gifts are revealed that have been chosen to delight the heart of the one who gives and the one who receives. The Bible tells us that all God's creation waited with the same feeling of excitement as his Son came into the world to be the best gift ever given.

Christmas Morning:

The question that puzzled those who witnessed the first Christmas still leaves us wondering today. If God came into the world as King, why is the world still such a flawed place? If he brought peace on earth, why are troops still manning the battlefields throughout the world every Christmas Eve?

Jesus didn't resolve the world's problems, as some thought he would. His own disciples expected that he would ride into Jerusalem one day and take over the throne, as earthly kings had done before him. Instead he humbled himself and rode into Jerusalem on a little lowly donkey. Jesus said that his kingdom was not of this world and that he desired instead the thrones of the hearts of those who would humble themselves and crown him King of their lives.

Perhaps that is why the wonder of Christmas never ceases to amaze us. A tiny baby was born, walked among us, and then died a cruel death so that we can live eternally. That tiny baby revolutionized history forever. He turned the world upside down.

Mary treasured up all these things and pondered them in her heart.

LUKE 2:19

When the time had fully come, God sent his Son, born of a woman, born under law, to redeem those under law, that we might receive the full rights of sons. Because you are sons, God sent the Spirit of his Son into our hearts, the Spirit who calls out, "Abba, Father."

GALATIANS 4:4–6

What child is this, who, laid to rest

On Mary's lap, is sleeping?

Whom angels greet with anthems sweet,

While shepherds watch are keeping?

This, this is Christ the King,

Whom shepherds guard and angels sing:

Haste, haste to bring Him laud,

The Babe, the Son of Mary!

So bring Him incense, gold, and myrrh,

Come peasant king to own Him,

The King of kings, salvation brings,

Let loving hearts enthrone Him.

Raise, raise the song on high,

The Virgin sings her lullaby:

Joy, joy, for Christ is born,

The Babe, the Son of Mary!

TRADITIONAL ENGLISH CAROL

Have the children make unique tree ornaments using photos of family members. Save the round metal ends from juice cans that have finished edges. Paste a photo of a family member on one side and cut a circle of colorful wrapping paper or felt, or an old Christmas card, for the other side. Glue a piece of lace, ribbon, or yarn around the outside edge of the circle, with a couple of inches left over to form a hanging loop. These make wonderful craft gifts for children to give grandparents.

For a Christmas Day table centerpiece using family photos, use last year's Christmas cards that have nice heavy paper and framed borders. For each card, cut out the centers, leaving the border, and insert a photo with a size that matches the opening. Tape or glue the card shut to act as a photo frame. Attaching a piece of cardboard cylinder from paper product

FAMILY FUN

rolls to the back of the "photo frame" will help it stand up. Place cards among evergreen branches. Add some tall candles and ribbon to complete the display.

Personalized snow globes are fun to make. They can be used as place cards, as a centerpiece, or in each child's room as a personal Christmas remembrance. Choose empty jars with nice tight lids and fill them with distilled water. Add a couple drops of glycerin to the jar, then sprinkle in a teaspoon or so of colored glitter. Glue small plastic toys to the inside of the jar's lid with epoxy glue, and allow the glue to dry thoroughly. Screw the lids tightly onto the jars, and turn them upside down to let the "snow" glitter fall onto the toys. Use stick-on letters to put each person's name on the snow globes if you want to use them as place cards.

CHAPTER 15

God's Great Gift

Christmas is a good time for giving. After all, we are celebrating the greatest gift ever given—God's Son.

God's great gift was first of all a gift of love to an unworthy world. He gave not because he had to, but because he loves us. And our giving should reflect his love. If we can keep that perspective—especially in the minds of our children—this can be one of the most blessed and enjoyable aspects of the holiday.

It isn't easy to keep one's perspective so focused. Christmas has become too commercial, too carefully merchandised, and too crassly materialistic to lend itself to teaching any spiritual truth about giving. Every year at Christmas, the buying frenzy gets worse.

I would like very much to pull the plug on the world's party, because I'm convinced there's an even better way to celebrate Christmas—one that's full of true joy and gladness, not the silly frivolity and careless gaiety most people settle for.

It begins, of course, with realizing the true significance of Jesus' birth. That means we must see beyond the familiar elements of Christmas and realize that at its heart Christmas is a celebration of the incarnation of God. If you see what Christmas really means, your immediate response will be worship.

JOHN F. MACARTHUR, *The Miracle of Christmas: God with Us*

God's Great Gift:

"The Twelve Days of Christmas" is a song about giving. However, it has another, more interesting meaning. It is a song of coded symbols to help English Catholics learn their catechism lessons in secret during the oppression of the sixteenth to nineteenth centuries when Protestants ruled England. In the Family Fun section, you'll find the words and meaning of the song.

Jesus was born into a land where people were persecuted for their faith. Persecution still happens today and many Christians in various countries are still in danger because of their belief in Jesus. Whatever gifts we open under our trees this Christmas morning, let's remember to be thankful for the greatest gift of all. Jesus didn't come to sit on a throne and rule us. He came to bring pure love and simple peace into our hearts and homes by the gift of his presence. As we celebrate his gift to us, we can be very thankful that in this country we are free to worship as we choose, and we can remember those members of the Christian family all over the world who embrace Christianity at the risk of persecution. We may think that one person can't do a lot to change the world, but a prayer has more power than we can ever imagine. On Christmas, our hearts unite in one voice and one desire with hundreds and thousands of others as we pray that those who suffer might be set free.

*G*od so loved the world that he gave his one and only Son, that whoever believes in him shall not perish but have eternal life.

JOHN 3:16

*W*ho, being in very nature God, did not consider equality with God something to be grasped, but made himself nothing, taking the very nature of a servant, being made in human likeness.

PHILIPPIANS 2:6–7

*T*hanks be to God for his indescribable gift!

2 CORINTHIANS 9:15

On the first day of Christmas,
My true love gave to me:
A partridge in a pear tree.

On the second day of Christmas,
My true love gave to me:
Two turtledoves, and a partridge ... etc.

On the third day of Christmas,
My true love gave to me:
Three French hens, two turtledoves ... etc.

On the fourth day of Christmas,
My true love gave to me:
Four calling birds, three French hens ... etc.

On the fifth day of Christmas,
My true love gave to me:
Five golden rings ... etc.

On the sixth day of Christmas,
My true love gave to me:
Six geese a-laying ... etc.

The Twelve
Days of
Christmas

On the seventh day of Christmas,
My true love gave to me:
Seven swans a-swimming … etc.

On the eighth day of Christmas,
My true love gave to me:
Eight maids a-milking …etc.

On the ninth day of Christmas,
My true love gave to me:
Nine ladies dancing … etc.

On the tenth day of Christmas,
My true love gave to me:
Ten lords a-leaping … etc.

On the eleventh day of Christmas,
My true love gave to me:
'Leven pipers piping … etc.

On the twelfth day of Christmas,
My true love gave to me:
Twelve drummers drumming … etc.

TRADITIONAL ENGLISH CAROL

Read through the song and the following information as a family. Discuss each part of the information. Get your children to tell you if the message is cleverly disguised. Ask them about secret codes they have had. Ask them what code they would use if they wanted to pass the good news about Jesus to someone else without everyone knowing what they were saying.

The repeated phrase "a partridge in a pear tree" in "The Twelve Days of Christmas" refers to Jesus.

Just as a partridge will put itself in danger to lead predators away from its chicks by pretending to have an injured wing, Jesus took our sins on himself and saved us by his sacrifice. Throughout this song that seems only to tell about giving gifts on Christmas, symbols tell the full story of Jesus' life and the great gift of his love. Let's look at some of the symbols.

God himself is the generous "true love" who gives good gifts to his people.

FAMILY FUN

Two turtledoves stand for the Old and New Testaments.

Three French hens represent faith, hope, and love that never fails.

Four calling birds are the four gospels in the New Testament: Matthew, Mark, Luke, and John.

Five golden rings symbolize the first five books of the Old Testament.

Six geese a-laying stand for the six days of God's creation of the world.

Seven swans a-swimming recall the seven gifts of the Holy Spirit.

Eight maids a-milking represent the eight Beatitudes of Christ's teaching in Matthew.

Nine ladies dancing symbolize nine types of angels.

Ten lords a-leaping indicate the Ten Commandments.

Eleven pipers piping are for the eleven faithful Apostles.

Twelve drummers drumming stand for the twelve elements of faith in the Apostles' Creed.

Sources

Joy Jacobs, *"God Became a Baby,"* Used by permission.

John F. MacArthur, *The Miracle of Christmas: God with Us* (Grand Rapids: Zondervan, 1989).

Ray Vander Laan, *Echoes of His Presence,* (Grand Rapids: Zondervan, 1998)